IRISH RECIPES

We offer in this little book a collection of some very old and famous recipes from Ireland. Some of these date back several hundred years and therefore not only give a taste of traditional Irish cooking but in some way a sense of our past.

   We have combined each recipe featured in this book with an illustration by a young Irish illustrator, Niamh O'Donnell.

Joe Reynolds

Little Books of Ireland

BROTCHÁN FOLTCHEP

2 lb Leeks
2 oz. Oatmeal
2 pt. Milk
Knob of Butter
Parsley
Salt and Pepper

COOK the oatmeal in the milk. Chop the leeks and mix with oatmeal. Add the butter. Cook for an hour. Season and garnish with chopped parsley.

COCKLE SOUP

2 pts. of Cockles
1 Stick of Celery
1 oz. Flour
1 oz. Butter
1 pt. Water
1 pt. Milk
Parsley

BOIL the cockles in cold water until they open. De-beard and shell them. Reserve the liquid. Make a roux with the flour and butter. Mix in the liquid and the milk. Add the chopped celery and simmer for half an hour. Add the cockles to the soup and sprinkle with parsley. Cook gently for a few minutes and serve.

COLCANNON

½ lb Cabbage
3 lb Potatoes
Small Onion
Butter
Salt and Pepper

BOIL the cabbage. Cook the potatoes and mash well. Chop up the cabbage and mix with potatoes. Cook chopped onion gently in butter until soft and stir in to the potatoes and cabbage mixture. Serve with a well of butter in the middle of each mound.

DUBLIN CODDLE

1 lb Pork Sausages
2 lb Thick Slices of Steaky Bacon
3 lb Potatoes
1 lb Onions
½ Pint water

DICE the bacon in two inch square pieces. Boil
with the sausages for five minutes. Drain and
place in an oven proof dish. Cover with thickly-
sliced potatoes, the onions and the water.
Sprinkle with parsley and cook in a moderate
oven for an hour.

CRUBIN

Pickled Pig's Feet
Water

ALLOW two pig's feet per person. Cover the trotters and bring slowly to the boil. Simmer for three hours. Serve hot with soda bread.

OYSTERS AND GUINNESS

4-6 Oysters per person
1 Lemon
Guinness

To open the shellfish place the oysters on a tea-towel, flat side up. Look for a chink or crevice in the shell at the narrow, hinged end. Insert oyster knife or chisel and press, turn, and lever upwards. Keep at it – it will open. Then insert a clean knife and cut the oyster away from the top shell. Serve immediately, chilled, with wedges of lemon and a glass of Guinness.

GRUNT SOUP

12 Grunts
(the young of Perch)
Flour
Scallions
1½ pt. Water
Butter
Salt and Pepper

CLEAN and scale the grunts. Simmer in water until tender. When cooked remove the skin and bones from the fish. Add chopped scallions to the fish stock and cook for fifteen minutes. Add the butter and thicken with flour. Finally, add fish meat and bring to the boil. Season and serve.

BOILED BACON AND CABBAGE

2 lb Piece of Boiling Bacon
1 Cabbage
Water

COVER Bacon with water and bring to the boil.
Cook the chopped Cabbage in the Bacon water
for 10 minutes and serve with the sliced hot
Bacon.

DRISHEEN

2 pt. Sheeps Blood
¼ lb Breadcrumbs
1 pt. Water
2 pt. Milk
1 lb Mutton Suet
2 tsp. Salt

STRAIN the blood and mix with all the other ingredients. Stand for one hour. Then simmer for three quarters of an hour. Cut into pieces and serve hot.

IRISH STEW

2 lb Brest of Mutton
2 lb Potatoes
1 lb Onions
1 pt. Water
Salt and Pepper

DICE the meat and place in a stewing pan with the sliced potatoes and onion, season, and add the water. Bring to the boil and simmer for an hour. When cooked, serve the meat surrounded by potatoes and onion.

CARRIGEEN MOSS

½ oz. Carrigeen Moss
2 tblsp. Sugar
1½ pt. Milk
Lemon Rind

WASH the moss. Bring slowly to the boil with the milk and lemon. Add the sugar. Strain into a wetted mould. When set, turn out and serve with stewed fruit.

PIGS HEAD BRAWN

1 Small Pig's Head and Tongue
2 Pig's Feet
2 Onions
Cloves
Mixed Herbs
Mace
Peppercorns

CLEAVE the head in two, removing the eyes, and brains and any gristle. Wash well. Scrub the feet. Cover the meat with water and add the herbs and spices. Simmer for six hours on a low heat until the meat is tender. Remove the meat from the bones. Reduce the liquid. Remove the skin from the tongue and slice. Fill mould with the chopped meat, packing it well. Add a little stock from the pot, if too dry. Then weight the top of the mould and allow to cool. When cold turn out and slice and serve.

FLUMMERY

Oatmeal
Water

SOAK the Oatmeal in water in a wide deep dish for 12 hours. Strain and stand again in water for 12 hours. Strain oatmeal. Bring to the boil, stirring continually until it thickens. Pour into dishes and let it set. Serve cold with cider and sugar.

NETTLE BROTH

2 pints of Nettle Tops
2 lb Boiling Beef
Scallions
A Cup of Barley
Salt and Pepper

BRING the meat and barley to the boil. Simmer on a low heat for two hours. Add the chopped scallions and nettles, and cook for another hour. Season to taste.

CHAMP

5 lb Potatoes
Scallions
½ Pint Milk
Butter
Salt and Pepper

COOK the potatoes and mash well. Heat the milk and chopped scallions. Then mix into the potatoes. Season and serve hot, with a large knob of butter in the centre of each plateful. Eat champ from the outside in, dipping each forkful into the well of melted butter.